Hood Holy

Lymandia Allen

Presentation by *BookLeaf Publishing*

Web: www.bookleafpub.com

E-mail: info@bookleafpub.com

ISBN: 9789357214308

First edition 2022

I dedicate this book to my sons: Tyree and D'Ari, my audience, my critics and my loves.

ACKNOWLEDGEMENT

I thank God for this opportunity.
I'd like to acknowledge my best friend on this earth, Vicki Hampton, who always believed that I could do this. Also, Kofi Averett, who would always ask if I finished the book and accepted no excuses. Thank you both.

PREFACE

From time to time, I'd often question myself as to who I am as a person, a woman. These poems touch on so many aspects of growing, it is my hope that you find yourself growing with me, and embracing your greatness.

Real Friend

While everybody is keeping it "100"
I'll go ahead and keep it a "G"
I have a thing about being fake,
so it's best to keep it real with me

Who I am is who I am
No matter the situation I'm in
So if you're going to be a part of this friendship
You'll have to be genuine

Have a real concern about my issues
As I make time for yours too
Don't brush me off or push me aside
because you don't like what I say to you

When we're together you're all smiles and you
have so much to say,
But I've learned you do that to push your agenda
And then act as if I'm in the way

It's iron sharpening iron, it takes correction and
maturity to grow
Things will not always go your way
You'll pluck away those seeds before you can
sow

I can be a real friend and have your back
It's so sad, you never took the time to see
My God revealed so many things about you
And you should have been more careful with me

That Ole Thing

That ole thing tried to come back, and he used to
smell so sweet
All he had to do was walk past me and my knees
would get so weak

That ole thing tried to come back, and it used to
get in my head
Stirred up my thoughts, like it was stirring up
coffee and twist the words I said

That ole thing tried to come back, and it used to
make my skin crawl,
Tore away at my emotions so much that I felt
like I was climbing a wall
I just couldn't wrap my head around why it
played so many tricks,
but I couldn't get enough of that ole thing
I always just needed one more fix

Of that ole thing, that had me by a string,
dangling in the wind,
 I was so comfortable with how it treated me
I somehow thought it was my friend

That ole thing tried to come back, and this time I
saw from down the street,
Singing the same old tune and even shuffling its
feet
But you see, I got a new thing now and my old
thing can't compete
Cause in my new thing I found rest in His arms,
and He gives me sweet sleep

When that ole thing tries to come around, my
new thing gives me a way of escape
You see, I have to hold tightly to my new thing
because this is for my soul's sake

Every now and then that ole thing tries to come
around just to see if he can get in
My new thing gives me grace for that, and
mercy says never again

And moment by moment the memory of that ole
thing will fade and pass away
See, there are no frets or anxieties with my new
thing because He's there every step of the way

So we've danced our last dance ole thing and
you can sing your song on your way out the door
I choose to hold tight to my new thing, and I just
don't need you anymore

Broken

My enemy was not supposed to look like you
you were supposed to be my closest friend
We were to have each other's back through
whatever
it's so unnecessary how this ends

My enemy was supposed to have horns, you see
And was never to take me by surprise
But it had a warm smile with inviting words and
big, beautiful brown eyes

And though I recognize that it's a spirit and will
find the closest one to you to use
I never, in my wildest dreams, thought that he
could use you

The one who made me feel special
The one that I let in,
The one who held my heart in his hands
Yet, you'd hurt it again and again

I'd still come back to you because I thought my
heart couldn't let you go
But when you began to talk down to me
Something inside let me know

That I could have all the care and love in the
world for you
But my presence wasn't doing the trick

So I took my cares and my love and put it away
because hanging around was making my soul
sick

My heart has never felt the pain that it feels now
 but this one thing I know to be true
That ole enemy will use the ones we love the
most and this time he used you

Torn

Torn without the evidence of a rip or tear
Torn between what's in front of me and what's
promised to always be there
Torn between the touch I felt so long ago and the
embrace that I engage in now
Torn with my feelings in a knot
And I just don't know how
I became torn

Done

So easy for some, but I was so done

Done with looking for someone to spend my
time with
Done with making plans and listening to
promises that wouldn't produce
I am tired

So done with the thought that I'm what's wrong,
When it was you, who was insecure all along

You'd say, "You're such a good woman"
And to some degree, it's true
But it was never my problem that I was too good
for you

That my independence was scary and made you
self-conscious
And my honesty forced you to mature
My intellect made you think, yet inside you
remained unsure

So done with putting together pieces
Of what the ones before me broke
So done with putting hope in what's hopeless

And looking like a joke

I'm DONE

Crown

I took it off, I put it down
Somehow, I forgot I was worth the crown
That it was worth the time and energy
God used when He created me
I forgot to be grateful for the gift inside
I let pride get in the way and I put it aside
The purpose never changed, neither did God's
plan
So the crown finds its place, upon my head
again

Look Back

Don't let your history be a mystery wrapped up
in what used to be

Back in the day is what they say but that day is
now
Make your mark, ignite the spark that places you
among the renown
You're not a relic, but relevant
Your heritage is your inheritance
 Add on to pass on
With your walk and Christ, this future is bright
Regardless of where you come from

Saint

I ain't no Saint
But his love still gets me high and causes me to
examine my purpose
And not just figure out ways to get by

But I'm telling you, I ain't no saint
Innocence is far from me, a new smell gone
away,
But he still whispers to me in my darkest
moment, because of His promise to never leave
or forsake

But child, I ain't no Saint
Yet, the Son still shines my way
In Him, lies my only hope and he holds my
forever in a day
While the cool breeze of His breath caress the
lilies of the field,
and from the ground the birds do feed
My helper, my keeper, my everything
He still supplies all that I need

But I'm trying to tell you
I ain't no Saint

Though my soul sings, my heart loves and my
mind retraces the day that we met
He has always known where I've been, and He'll
always know where I'll be
See, because of who He is
He makes me a Saint and He's the one who
makes me free

Don't Judge Me

Please don't judge me

With fake smiles and forced grins
You haven't lived my life or even been where
I've been

Where my light shines brighter than the morning
sun
To the dimness of darkness, where there was
almost none

So how would you know, what it is that I should
know
When what you don't know is me
You know what you've seen and gave attention
to what you heard
But you look at me and still fail to see
 Me

Hood Holy

So I say I'm hood Holy
' Cause I will still throw these hands,
But I'd rather raise them up
And give honor to the man

To the one who tells me that I'm worth it,
With each new day he brings
Who showed me that no matter the problem,
He's the solution to everything

And I say that I'm hood Holy
because I've been caught wrong and yes, I've
even cussed
But even in my hood holiness
I've learned that I don't have to fight but so much

I have no point to prove and I don't need my
word to make a case
With the Lord being my defense
The naysayers and haters are so easy to face

Because no weapon formed can harm me
You know, I'm covered on every side

So I just sit in my heavenly placed passenger
seat
And enjoy this Hood Holy ride

Because I'm Hood Holy

Business

Because it's my business,
I know what I want

Because it's my business,
I never have to flaunt,

Because it's my business,
my moves belong to me

Because it's my business,
I'm the only one who needs to see

Because it's my business,
I mind the business that pays me
And me, minding my business is always free

My Lane

I'm really in a good place
exploring my space, setting my pace
And running my race

I have no room to complain
Because I stay in my lane

I have had situations arise and lost sight of the
prize
And at times let things get me down,

But when I look back now, my feet was on solid
ground,
I just got caught up and stepped out of bounds

Hate Mail

I just want to say thank you for all that you do
I wouldn't be where I am, if it wasn't for you

For all the times you threw salt, making my
flavor oh, so sweet
It's because of you, I win, even when it looks
like defeat

For all those times you said my name, so that
strangers could hear
For some thereby have entertained angels
unaware

For all the times you lied on me, trying to make
my life so hard
All you did was bring me closer to the Most
High God
Who is adding more angels to strengthen my
line of defense
You've said my name one too many times, but
I've been blessed ever since

I thank you for all the fake smiles, behind them
are plots and schemes

Because it kept me focused on my assignment
and I'm so much closer to living my dreams

So here's to you hater, don't stop doing those
things you do
Every time I sign my million-dollar signature, I
will be thinking of you

If

I use to wonder if through space and time
I'd find a place inside your mind

If for a second, a minute, an hour in parts
was my imaged etched in your heart

If starting anew is better the second time
Because of learning from the mistakes made
from moments behind

Looking through a different lens,
Seeing things afresh,
Attempting to start again, with the one you loved
best

Or reliving a pattern, with the one you fell
foolish for
Nah Sis, let that be over and slam the hinges off
that door

Accountability

It's my fault
I didn't recognize my worth and I let him get
close enough to touch my emotions and get
caught up

It's on me, because he truly meant nothing that
he said,
But somehow it became a melody in my head

It had a nice rhythm and is sounded so sweet
I remember when it required so much to get me

I slipped up, I didn't get it; but you know I
usually do
I'm usually on point about not looking like the
fool

But this one is on me
It did what it does because I opened the door
I crushed its head and slammed it shut
And we can't hear him whisper anymore

I needed to own up to it, this can no longer set
on the shelf
God has so much more in store for me,

So, I must first apologize to myself

I'm Sorry

Who Am I

I am the world's eight wonder
Formed from the rib of man
I am as bright as the stars
And as plenteous as the sand
Given as a precious gift
Made perfect by His hand

I am the "Muse" to "ic"
I am the rhyme to reason
I am the winter, spring,summer and fall; the
beauty of every season

I am the skip on your step
And the joy in your laughter
I am the calm before the storm
And the blessings that come after

I am the strong tower
On me, you can lean
I'll strengthen the hedge of protection
And close the gaps in between

I use His words to move mountains
And calm the seas
Restore sight to the blind

And cure disease

At night it gives me sweet sleep
And in the morning, it commands my day
His Word builds my arsenal
For the giants that I am sure to slay

I am as sweet as they come
And as tough as they get
But you ain't seen nothin'
'Cause God's not done with me yet

I'm not saying that its easy
But with Him, nothing's too hard
Not only did He make me phenomenal
He calls me a woman of God

I Know How to Pray

He's done so much for me even when I get in my
own way
His words flow freely from my lips
I know how to pray

I worry not about worldly circumstance
And all my crooked places, you've made straight
The angels hearken and to the voice of the Lord
Because I know how to pray

I'm not moved by the terror at night
Or the darts that fly by day
You have covered me under your mighty shadow
Because it's for your protection I prayed

I can look back over my life
And see how you've always made a way
There's nothing too hard for you and me
Because I know how to pray

This Place

I have found my perfect place
Which provides for me the proper headspace
And I know myself in such a way
That no matter what others think they know or
say
God's Word will always carry the weight

The weight of He'll never forsake or leave
That even when in my valley,
He's right there with me
That when I'm in the thick of it and it seems like
He's gone without a trace
I can bow my head before Him and diligently
seek his face

The weight that makes me the head and not the
tail
And even in delays, all is well
That places me above and not beneath,
And keeps the enemy smothered under my feet

In Him, I abide in my peaceful place and every
blessing belongs to me
No matter what others say or think
It's the weight of His Word that makes me free

Unmistakable

I am apparent and obvious; easy to be seen
I stand out, I'm different, there's a patent on me

I'm distinguished by nature
Unlike the others and not the same
I am distinct and evident
The world will know my name

I am created by design
Established by His grace
Planted here on purpose;
A part of a heavenly race

I'm without a doubt rare
And it's with true certainty
That His way is perfect and there was no
mistake
When God created me

Worth

The day it left, I couldn't catch my breath
My wind was gone and the grip escaped my feet
I felt my heart pound, as my tears hit the ground
And the pit of my soul did weep

My train of thought jumped track,
As I tried to think back to pinpoint what wrong
did I do

Then the image appeared
Apparent and clear
I did wrong by choosing you

I didn't allow you to seek Him
And in Him find me
I didn't let Him keep me covered
And I exposed the mystery

The mystery of my worth
You'd discover, what I was yet to know
That knowing my value would give me power
Enough power to let you go

So you kept it
The secret and the web began to spin

I was trapped, not because of who you are
But the deceit, that I let in

Then it left, and is so long gone
That I have not one tear to cry
I found my worth and this no longer hurts
So with a smile, I can say goodbye

Thank You

Heavenly Father,
I just want to say thank you
For sending you Son to die for me
to forgive me of my every sin so, that I could be
free

I just want to say thank you
For the morning sun that rise
For the birds that serenade me in song
as I open my eyes,

I just want to say thank you
For putting a smile on my face
For leading me and guiding me
as I run this faith race

I just want to say thank you,
because without you, there is no me
If I had not found you, I truly don't know where
I'd be

I just stopped by to say thank you
Because I feel it's something that you should
always hear
through the stress and strife and busy-ness of life

We often forget that you're right there
Thank You
Amen

www.ingramcontent.com/pod-product-compliance
Lightning Source LLC
LaVergne TN
LVHW010927200726
843509LV00013B/2119

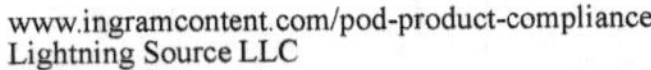